$GOD \times 0 =$ EVERYTHING

THE DIVINE EQUATION

To my daughter, Arolyn...
May you always know the Purpose
of the Divine Equation in Whom
God has created you to be!

To the reader,

I'm so blessed to share this book with you. I've learned through the years that God generally doesn't release you to His precious people (that would be you) absent trials by fire. Because He loves you most, extraordinary callings aren't tried through ordinary fires.

To that end I'll just say "Ouch! – Your Father Really Loves You!"

My prayer is that you are encouraged... know that He sees you... He has you ... His plan for you is awesome... So, trust Him with you!

Be Blessed,

       La Tonya

CHAPTER ONE
"YOU GOT TO BE KIDDING ME!"

I've just been notified that one of my "amazing opportunities" has collided with a brick wall. September 10, 2015, at approximately 1:15 a.m., I awoke to check my phone and saw the "You're No Longer Welcome Here" message. The reason - I did not meet my funding deadline and was, therefore, "No Longer Welcomed".

I had been diligently preparing now for just shy of a month for this fashion event – designing, pattern and garment construction, deconstruction, reconfiguring pattern sizes to the representative's new specs, material purchasing, learning advertisement creation software, creation of additional garments for promo-purposes, etc.

"Just suck it up and do it – it's just part of the process," I thought to myself and resumed focus.

The time frame to get my garments completed was very short compared to that of the other emerging designers. I didn't have the full fee but the representative graciously extended the deadline. I learned the day of the promo shoot it was canceled. Therefore, the revised fee due date and promo shoot scheduled last week was rescheduled for today! Yes, the very day that I received the – well you know.

This may seem to you, the reader, just a matter of my not being prepared to meet the opportunity. Besides, fabric is not that expensive, right?

I see your points and will be the first to admit this event led me to some swift self-examination. I asked "What did I do?" and "What didn't I do?" You've asked the same questions of yourself when positive-moving events take a hard-left (screeching off the road into a big muddy ditch).

What if I told you that:

1) I'm a single mother;

2) I've been unemployed for almost two

years now;

3) I have no steady stream of income;

4) I'm building a business and

5) I am operating on a Daily Faith?

Then that fabric becomes way more expensive - that time has drastically increased in value and the loss of that "amazing opportunity" is now more than a mere glancing blow. Not to mention I could have allotted all that energy towards other productive and lucrative purposes – perhaps. More importantly, I felt I disappointed the people who invested in me.

"So, what am I going to do now?" you ask.

Well, the process of recounting past struggles and remembering how God answered has already begun. So, I'm going to share with you a few of those events while I wait on Him to show up and miraculously answer again.

Journal Entry/September 8, 2015

Up at 2:00 a.m. Still up... Impressed to write my book...in 7 days...

Lord help me... perhaps God's instruction to pull back this past week

from "Woman, Warrior, Friend" (WWF) was to refocus me to this

book... God x 0=Everything... I'm up...getting ready for fashion

event...Listened to Sonya Ramsey on Periscope – she gave quick

bullet-point rundown of how to self-publish...going to get that

down...it's time...Shirley (my Step-mom) will be ecstatic ...

Thank you Lord! ~end~

Okay so let's first address the title *God x 0 = Everything.* More than likely, when you read this, one of your immediate responses was "what in the world is she talking about?" - followed by "that makes absolutely no sense at all!" and you would be right!

It makes no sense that I would have absolutely nothing and still have all I needed... It makes no sense that my friend Sunshine and I stood stymied in my front yard keenly aware that though I had no money my electricity was still on... It makes no sense that at the point when I needed gas for my car – she called to ask if I needed gas for my car... It just makes no sense at all - that is from a purely "practical" perspective. However, note that when "God" is in the equation – the beginning of the equation – He shows Himself strong and everything that is seemingly impossible is turned on its ear!

When "God" shows up - it is nothing less than Amazing!

For those skeptics out there – I've got witnesses who have watched the hand of God move and can testify for themselves to the same. They have graciously given me permission to use their names and I appreciate them. Allow me to put a *pin* right here because you, yourself have seen the hand of God move. You may have dismissed it as a fluke or relegated it to "luck" – but you have witnessed it – either in your own life or in someone else's.

Now that we've gotten that out of the way - let's begin. I'll begin with an end – my divorce.

I came out of my divorce with the biggest blessing and an empty bucket - my daughter the former and my bank account the latter. I was left with "0" dollars which gave me no choice but to rely on God for everything.

Let me suggest that before and after you read each chapter – rehearse in your mind that amazing equation *God x 0 = Everything*.

Throughout this read, you'll find posts and lyrics of various musical selections I've written. I know this is kind of different - it's meant to be. So be sure to take time to reflect on these entries. You may also look up and download the music from most any online digital music source. This is an *interactive* journey of encouragement. You ready?... Let's go!

Letter of Encouragement (Lyrics)

Thought I'd send a letter to you – of Encouragement

Just in case your head is hanging down low

And you feel your call is a lost cause and you find you have no

strength at all

Just in case you feel a little low – ready to go

And you're thinking "I can't do this at all"

You need reminding of a Loving God

Who's there when you call

I know it gets hard sometimes – wrestling with things on your mind

Grappling with insecurity – questioning what you're meant to be

For you I pray that the light of God will brighten your way

Follow you with mercy and grace - and your strength He will renew

I've been thinking about you constantly – thinking about you

You're on my mind – thinking about you – all the time!

~end~

Now, Be Encouraged My Friend!

CHAPTER TWO
"HOUSE TO HOUSE"

One of the most challenging issues stemming from the divorce would be finding a home. Because I was a stay-at-home mom I had no job and thus no income. But – I had to find a place for my daughter. I recalled previously driving through, what seemed to be, a very nice neighborhood of duplexes with an old friend. She had been looking for a place of her own at that time.

I got on the computer, did a search and found both the duplex address and the management company. There was a vacancy – Excellent! Made that call and found out the rent and deposit amount. Good! Now came the hard part – I had no money!

I contacted the pastor of the church I was attending and explained that I needed funds to just get into the space. He was aware of my situation because we had talked about it on several occasions and asked me to give him time to think about it. His suggestion was that my daughter and I move in with some church members. That was a nice plan, but I knew that wasn't God's direction for me. I asked him to allow me time to consider it – hung up the phone and bowed my head to pray. It was more like my head just dropped and I asked God for help.

I raised my head up and continued my search – I heard "Call Alvin". What? … No, I'm not going to call him. Alvin was a dear friend with whom I played tennis. He, like the pastor, was aware of my predicament and was part of a small group of people who was a source of encouragement during some emotionally-rough events. I heard it again – to call him. No… I wasn't about to call him and ask for money. No way! Ring, went the phone… I answered - it was Alvin calling me!

"Hey La Tonya, what're you doing?"

"I'm on the computer looking for apartments."

"You are?"

"Yes."

"Good, you can't stay there."

"I know…"

Then he asked, "La Tonya, do you need money to help you get a place?"

How could he know that – well other than my unemployed status – but how could he know that was my specific need at that very moment? There was no denying my heavenly Father's hand in this. Overwhelmed, I answered "yes" and was thankful he couldn't witness the hot tears that rolled down my face.

"Okay, what do you need?"

I told him how much and for where and quickly added that I would pay him back.

"No problem at all. Don't worry about it – pay me when you can."

I cannot adequately express how grateful I was. So significant was that gift – an unsolicited one at that. It is amazing how God cares for us through others.

The next order of business was to get to the property management office right away to sign a lease before my credit report scores got any lower. I had no monies so everything that was under my name – even credit cards used for the household – wasn't being paid. My daughter and I went to the management office – and I warned the clerk that due to my situation, my scores may be "kinda ugly".

I waited patiently (what else could I do, right?) for the report to come in and the lady's review. She looked at me and said, "They aren't bad at all!"

My soft response was "Really?" but in my head I screamed, "WHAT!?!!!"

She handed me the report to read, quickly completed the rental agreement forms and gave me the keys. I thanked her and we walked out of the office.

Internally celebrating, I stood for a moment and slowly exhaled. My eyes scanned the panoply of the crowded parking lot. I took a deep breath and nodded my head. An onlooker would have attributed that gesture to perhaps talking with my daughter. It was, in fact, an acknowledgment that though this battle was won I had to get ready for the next one.

Apparently, my application submission was timed just right and the credit scores I had worked hard to attain stood tall beautifully on the paper. But, I was well aware even though the "fall" hadn't manifested - it had already begun.

God was faithful in getting me a contract job where I worked as a paralegal "of sorts" for an attorney. I say "of sorts" because it wasn't a good fit – my skill set vs. her needs. She needed more of an administrator not a prognosticator. I'm grateful, though, for that short time spent. Then, I was hired full-time at a non-profit organization. Everything seemed to be on the up-tick. The search for our "home" continued.

CHAPTER THREE
"FALLING FROM ZERO"

There I was on the phone with my credit union account manager, trying to convince her that if she allowed me to continue making small payments, I would work hard to eventually "outrun" the accruing interest.

Didn't she know I had been a stay-at-home mom for five years and, in the aftermath of divorce, was left with no home and $0 in the bank? Didn't she know I was a single mother and had to start all over? Didn't she know I had just acquired this full-time job? Didn't she know I was a hard-worker?

All were rhetorical questions because she actually did know. I had opened my account with that institution when I was fourteen. My mother worked there as a teller and I kept my account even after she had passed. That was a twenty-two year old account. So, she was aware of all of the above and also well aware I would never catch up.

"La Tonya," she said "I'm going to do for you what needs to be done. You will not say 'close this account' so I'm closing it for you!"

"But my credit rating… everything I've worked hard for…"

"Honey-" I could hear a caring finality in her tone. "I understand and we know what has happened – this has to be done"

She was right. There was no other way. I said a quiet "okay" fully realizing that even if I hadn't acquiesced, her decision concerning what was best for me had already been made.

The last thing I heard her say was, "It will be alright."
"Thank you".

After hanging up the receiver, I got up, shut my office door laid my head on my desk and wept silently.

I wept because…
I knew I would need every advantage, credit and otherwise, to provide for my daughter.

I wept because…
I didn't go into a marriage thinking I would ever be here.

I wept because…
I had given my all (sold my home; left a career) and had nothing financially to show for it.

I wept because…
I had to start all over again, again.

I wept because I was exhausted, worn and empty.
I didn't know it was possible but I had fallen from zero.

Little did I know, that was the exact "position" necessary to be strengthened by God. His plan for me would continue to unfold as I walked this faith journey - day by day - one step at a time. He would be my source, my encourager, my all.

CHAPTER FOUR
"IT'S ABOUT GRACE"

My divorce left me with huge debt, plummeting credit and two cars. Don't get excited -neither of them worked well. I had a no-running old Ford Escort (the first car I ever bought) and a Honda we got for the bargain price of $200 because it was a casualty of a flood. The Honda was running but had no air conditioning which made the Oklahoma summer even more brutal – especially for my baby-girl riding in the backseat.

The Honda was showing severe signs of decline. It sounded as if it had a horrible case of the whooping cough and would sputter upon both starting and shutting down. That I needed a car wasn't a question – how would I ever qualify to purchase one was the real issue. My credit score was doing a "nose-dive" and there was no savings to speak of.

I began sensing that I needed to go to a Toyota dealership.

"What?" you ask.

Well, "What?" I asked too!

Again it was impressed upon me to go to a Toyota dealership. I was aware of only one such dealership solely because it was heavily advertised on television. As it turned out, I knew one of the salesmen! Obviously, this was the dealership (right?) so I drove down.

Nope, it wasn't the one.

They were kind, of course, and suggested I needed to focus my efforts on getting something bright, shiny and new. After checking my credit (I'm sure they did a double-take), they tried to "squeeze" me into a new "hot-rod" model.

"We can make the numbers work, don't worry about it" said the rather handsome-looking manager as he reclined in his chair.

(What? He *was* handsome. I'm just trying to tell you the story.)

My response - "Okay, how?"

I'd seen the numbers and it was going to take nothing less than a miracle to get me and my bad credit into a car – much less a newer model. He didn't make it work. Or rather, he didn't show me the working numbers. So my girl and I said our "thank you" and "goodbyes", got into our old Honda, rolled down our windows and headed home.

It bothered me that nothing came to fruition car-wise. Didn't I hear Him say go to a Toyota dealership? Am I just confusing myself and in the process lying on God? You know what happened next – a quick *Self-Examination*.

I spoke with my friend La Vern about my car woes. She gave me the name of a salesman who, she said, "had integrity and helped her brother out a lot." That was quite a recommendation coming from her because she's anything but willy-nilly with her accolades.

"Why not", I thought, "I need all he help I could get." Especially since it would seem watching too much television had compromised my ability to hear God's instructions clearly. (Yes, I know I could've just turned the TV off – that wasn't the point!)

She gave me the salesman's contact information and the dealership location. Get this – it was a Toyota dealership! If this doesn't intrigue you – believe me – I was intrigued enough for the both of us. I called him to set an appointment and headed out.

He was very kind. Turned out, he was a minister who was taking a sabbatical, of sorts, trying to "hear" God's direction for his ministry. (Maybe too much TV was crowding his mind also!) Again, he was very kind. Nevertheless, his kindness was no match for my plummeting credit. My credit score had acquired super-hero (or super-villain) status by then! I laugh now - but it's still not funny!

The salesman established that I had two cars for trade-in and said I would have to "settle" for a used vehicle. I remember telling him that all I cared about was that it ran well – it didn't have to be brand new.

He said "Okay, let's take a look at the list of used cars that we have available."

I sat at his desk to look through the list. They had quite a few used-car options. He would read the info and I would give the thumbs-up (mostly thumbs-down). Within a short period of time we had established a rhythm which was broken by his sudden silence.

"What's happening? - Did you find a good one?" I asked.

With an expression of incredulity on his face, he replied "I think so – it's a Volvo. But, I've never seen this listing before. It's in the back area now – getting cleaned before they bring it out. Do you want to see it?"

Absolutely, I wanted to see it. If I hadn't wanted to initially - his perplexed expression alone would have made me curious enough to go see it. The notion that this listing just "appeared" was the icing on the cake. Neither of us could wait – we all (my daughter was with me) had to see!

We had no idea what to expect. Then the salesman pointed to the car in the farthest bay. I saw her – and she was beautiful! The salesman looked at me and we both smiled knowingly. What did we know? We knew that God had chosen that vehicle specifically for me. He orchestrated the timing, place and people in order to bless me!

One of the other salesmen approached me and said, "You're the one getting that Volvo? That's a really nice car! I never even saw it on the list. If I had, I would have grabbed that one for sure."

Oh, I neglected to share the significance and my excitement of getting a "Volvo". No, I'm not a brand-slave so it wasn't because I wanted to reflect a certain image. One of my past co-workers drove an old Volvo. She explained that these cars have a steel bar that runs the length of the driver and passenger sides. This unique construction gives added protection in car crashes. I knew I wanted to drive this when I had a family. At that time, I was single and had no children (and no marriage prospect). That was over six years prior to my actually purchasing one. God remembered.

A friend came over to see the car – I expected her to be just as excited for me as I was. Her remark, "Your car is better than mine" told me otherwise. I chose to include this "friend's" remark to note here that not everyone will be joyous that God is blessing you –

especially if they consider themselves on a higher socio-economic (or other) status. What you must remember is that God sees and He rewards and He gives above all we can imagine.

We named her "Grace" – "Grey Grace", to be exact, because it was so clear that this vehicle was a manifestation of God's unyielding Grace towards us. Each day when I drive, I'm reminded of His mercy and grace that is running to overtake me! Sometimes when I'm feeling low, I have to slow my feelings down to recount to myself how He has shown the evidence of His love towards me.

CHAPTER FIVE
"GRACE OF A DIFFERENT COLOR"

I don't recall if it was kindergarten or first grade – but I do recall the fear. My Mom and I had moved to a new place about twenty minutes from Grandma's house – just over the highway. She was taking me to the bus stop. It was frightfully cold so I had on my hat, mittens, tights with socks and a fluffy coat.

It was an exciting morning. Everything was so bright - I had been talking all the way to the bus stop. Then Mom turned to me and said, "You have to stay *here* and wait for the bus – I have to catch that city bus to go to work." Only then did I take a real good look around to see where exactly "here" was.

Here was an old vacated office building with no roof or walls. The sound of the wind rattled the partial partitions, playing a cruel game of hide-and-seek. She watched as I looked around - waiting for me to take it in – awaiting my reaction. In retrospect – what could she have said?

I saw the bus pull up on the other side of the street. She must have seen the fear reflected in my eyes. As she positioned me into the inner-most corner of that dilapidated space, Mom hugged and told me she loved me and that I was not to come out from *here* until I see other children at the bus-stop. I nodded and said "yes ma'am."

I don't recall if the tears started before or after she left. But I watched her quickly walk away to cross that highway - to catch that bus - to go to that job that left me *here* all alone and so scared.

I hated that bus. I hated that highway. I hated this space. I hated my fear. I cried – quietly though because I didn't want anyone to hear me.

It seemed like forever before a few kids made it to the bus-stop. Only then did I come out. Safety – I was safe. A wonderful lady who lived across the street took notice and told my Mom I could stay in her home to wait for the bus. You see, her son, Michael was in my grade and he became a sort of "protector" of me. For example, he wouldn't let anyone cut line in front of me. That's important stuff in a child's life. This arrangement didn't last long because my Mom purchased her first car – a bright yellow Volkswagon Rabbit!

It had to be the most beautiful car I had ever seen – not because of its flair but because it meant we didn't have to impose on Mrs. Johnson any longer and the likelihood that I would have to endure being left alone like that again (in my mind) was impossible.

I've often reflected on that event in my adult life when

circumstances are such that I've been "left" alone or rejected. It's a reminder of God's protection even when I feel like an island – a deserted island at that.

My Mom and I talked about this event many years later. She asked if I cried. I told her yes. She said, "So did I".

I loved that bright yellow Volkswagon. For me, its color represented "hope". That feeling was mirrored at that dealership when I saw my Volvo. I've learned that *Grace* shows itself in many colors.

Are you rehearsing God x 0 = Everything?... Okay, just checking!

CHAPTER SIX
"EXCEPT THE LORD BUILD A HOUSE"

A place to call home was the focus. It was a blessing to find the duplex, however, we couldn't decorate and there was not much of a back yard to speak of. The entire kitchen shook whenever the garage door shut. Still, I was grateful to have a roof over our head. But, we needed a home. My girl was growing and I wanted a space that she could call her own – stability.

I had the privilege of having a good friend who was a realtor who, long before this time, would go with me and check out house listings I had found. Norman, who had helped sell the first home I purchased and my then husband's rental property, would trek out to these homes and acreages shaking his head at my persistence. One day he suggested I move to an area farther east where I could own land. I laughed at that notion. (How ironic that I would end up in that area – happily.)

I had moved from the duplex to a rental – farther east. If you've ever longed for your own stake in land, I don't have to tell you that it seemed like we resided in each rental property for a decade each. I had procured a job and was blessed with a good running automobile. Now, we needed a place to call home.

My daughter and I each wrote a list of what we wanted in our home. A weeping willow tree, walk-in closet and a wishing-well were a few items she listed. I wanted land, space, fence and a gas stove! Fire-Fire-Fire!!! So, on went the search for our home.

Norman and I had viewed many spots – one with a completely flooded basement to which he said "Hey you have your own built-in swimming pool!" (Gross); another that had bright orange shag carpet on the walls. We finally viewed one house that seemed to have potential. The layout was odd but doable – sunken living area made for easy entertainment. So we made an offer.

I must say, Norman was first a friend then my agent. And as such, would allow me room to "blow up" when the seller made "additional" requests. He knew I'd eventually calm down and then come to my senses. Apparently my tirades were amusing because more often than not he would be laughing hysterically when they subsided. Needless to say, I was not amused at his being amused!

One evening I received a call from Norman. He was in the office late working on my documents. We were in negotiations and it seemed that there was always one more thing that needed to be done or hashed out. I was becoming frustrated. He knew this and said after my mini-tirades, "You know I got you right?"

It was more of statement than a question.

"You got me?"

"Yes, I got you".

"Okay, I'm calm now."

He said okay and reminded me to check my email for the updated documents he had just e-mailed.

"Okay, I'll call you when I sign and upload them."

"La Tonya"…

That was odd. Norman rarely called me by my first name. Everything stopped and he had my full attention.

"Yes?" I waited for what was to follow – sensing it would be of grave importance.

After a few moments of silence he said, "Nothing - just let me know when you send the forms okay?"

"Okay"

I tried not to let my imagination run wild with concern, attempting to figure out what he possibly would have wanted to discuss, and scanned the forms. There's no way I could've known that, shortly after that telephone conversation, my friend entered the building's elevator to leave and suffered a severe stroke.

It was late - the building was closed. He was found by another realtor who decided to drop by the office.

Norman never recovered – nor did the negotiations for the house. It was hard to wrap my mind around the fact that I was most likely the last person he spoke to before the stroke.

If I had it to do all over again, I would tell him how grateful I was to have had a friend like him. He had been just that – a friend for over twenty years. I would tell him that I loved him. I'd told him that before but in retrospect not nearly enough.

I miss my friend.

I smile when I see where I am now, aware that the streams of homes he showed me were always due east. That's important because ultimately, God knew my heart – what I wanted in a home.

Norman had been showing me places that were just a stone's throw away from the place I would eventually call "home" - God had prepared an enormous faith adventure to get me there.

CHAPTER SEVEN
"WAKING UP"

I'd lost a good friend who was also my realtor. The dream of ever owning a home (again) felt utterly unattainable. Much more, the thought of starting over with another realtor – building that relationship – was disconcerting. It really didn't matter because nothing could happen until my credit was in-line. The search was halted – for a bit.

I signed up online for one of those free credit watch programs in order to monitor my progress. Progress was being made although very slowly. We moved from the duplex to a rental home. You guessed it – further east!

This was most timely because the management company was pressuring me to purchase the duplex. No way! That meant I was now on a month-to-month lease – which allowed perspective buyers (strangers) to enter and view the space. I was not a fan of that legally-allowed intrusion. Thankfully, we signed a lease for another rental property (transitioning east). It was timely. Thank God!

The credit monitoring program would send me monthly updates showing that slow (but sure) accent of my puny score. My excitement grew accordingly. I monitored the monitoring for the score to reach a specific number. As soon as it did, I picked up the phone and made a call to a lender.

This was the same process I undertook when I sought to purchase my first home. Before getting my hopes too high, I decided to pre-apply with a lender. It was best that I knew upfront what I would be approved for. Upon seeing that home I knew it was mine. So I made a full offer and got the seller to agree to 1) stop showing the home to others and 2) utilize one realtor for purposes of facilitating the sale and completing the necessary documentation only. She agreed. (Guess who that realtor was? - Norman)

The first lender I contacted could've just left me a message like "Are you crazy?" That was the sense I got from him when he explained my score was sub-par. That was perplexing because my monitoring service reflected I was good to go. A little dismayed but not daunted, I decided to give it another month and tried again.

This time the message was "You are crazy – don't waste my time crazy-lady!"

I contacted the monitoring service and learned that their numbers were a little inflated. Irate doesn't adequately convey how I felt. I'm sure I mulled over some choice words – none of them I'd care to recall at this moment.

Bigger frustration had set in because I was back to actively searching for a home and had been extremely excited about it. I kept looking though.

There was this listing that intrigued me. I had been watching it for a moment but dared not call the realtor. Felt I wasn't ready or rather my credit wasn't. One day I got up the nerve and convinced myself to call the listing's realtor. It sounded as if the home had everything I wanted. The agent was very kind and I explained that I was getting things in order and would call her soon to set up a viewing.

I'm not sure who recommended a different lender to me but I followed through. She did more than a cursory view of my credit – she delved into understanding why my scores were not getting higher. It was determined that an error in reporting was the issue. That was great except for the fact that it would take at least three or more months for the corrections to reflect in my scores. That meant waiting.

I was becoming more and more discouraged by the blocks that were being hurled in my path. Just how soon I would be able to move forward with the purchasing of *any* home was up in the air. Who knew? So hesitantly, I contacted the agent to let her know not to expect me anytime soon – if at all. She was gracious and said, "Well, if you ever want to just see it – call me and I'll make myself available."

One Saturday, a friend invited my daughter over for a play-date. She told me to just enjoy my day - she'd watch the girls. I drove around the area not far from the house we were renting – enjoying the land layout and the drive. It dawned on me that this area would be a good place to open a business so I began surveying the streets more closely.

I had been traveling due east for a time and came to a four-way stop. Wondering where on earth I was and unfamiliar with the area I finally decided to read the street sign. (Reading is a good thing!) The street was where the house was located! Yes, I did – headed right up the road to view the home for myself.

The sight of the home – the land – the location - made me cry. It was a beautiful space. I thought to myself "Whoever gets this home will be blessed!" This I felt so much so that I called and shared the same with the agent. She asked if I could wait so she could show me the property. I said yes – what did I have to lose (except more tears).

It was amazing and it felt like home. I met and spoke with the owners who were gracious and entertaining. They loved their home – you could feel it. I couldn't blame them.

I departed thinking to myself, "That one got away". However, I was so glad I got to see it. This was encouraging because it awakened the hope in me that God heard my prayer for a home. He did lead me to the street didn't He? I had met both the agent and homeowners but had no idea the significance of that meeting. It would soon be revealed.

CHAPTER EIGHT
"COLOR TO MY MELLOW"

That lender was right, it took a few months and I was in the zone or rather my credit score was. I had stable employment and was deemed a worthy risk. Thank God! After speaking with the agent, we determined that she would handle the entire transaction for both buyer and seller.

Now if any of you are familiar with the home-buying process you know there a costs involved – such as money you have to put out for termite and house inspections. No, they are not the same thing – I asked. We can't forget the down-payment and utility transfers as well.

On one particular evening, the agent informed me I had to pay $861 for the house inspection. I could've sworn she was speaking in a foreign language and asked her to repeat it. She did and then my response was "Hugh?" She repeated the same and I understood it clearly. What I didn't understand was "Why?" After ending the call, I slumped against my bathroom door.

Why was there always something else? - Why can't I get a break? - Why am I the one always struggling especially when I'm trying to do right? – Why, why, why... I was doing my best to have a full-on snotty-nose pity party. But my every attempt to wallow was countered with a memory flash of how God delivered. ("Amen" inserted right here is appropriate).

There was a Kung-Fu like battle going on in my mind – every thought of defeat was countered and subsequently crushed by a memory of deliverance. Punch and counter-punch kept alternating so much that I couldn't even squeeze out a small tear.

The realization that God wasn't allowing any attempts to abandon myself to a pool of pity made me laugh out loud. Shaking my head, I looked up and said, "You just won't let me have this whining party - you just keep adding color to my mellow!"

So I did what naturally came next – I wrote a song "Color to My Mellow" (to be released Summer/2016), took a shower, went to bed and thanked Him for the answer that surely was on its way. He is God – so it had to be!

Glenda, a co-worker was in my office and I was explaining the house inspection fiasco. She was a believer and we surmised together that God was going to do something miraculous – because only He could! The agent called while she was still in my office.

Apparently, the house inspector was in the process of certifying other inspectors and wanted to use my property for the training. Since he was paid by the students, my fee was dismissed. In effect, I would have over ten people inspecting my property. That was an unbelievable answer to prayer even though I still had to pay for the termite inspection. (Remember they're two different things)

But wait – there's more!

The agent told me what my reduced inspection charges would be. I confirmed the amount, wrote it down and thanked her. Glenda watched me write the information and a look of astonishment spread over her face.

"Don't you see it?" she asked after I'd hung up with the agent.

"What?"

She pointed to the figure I had written down. "Look at the number – He turned it around!"

As she turned the paper around I began to see... the new amount due was now $168.

Holy, Holy-A God Like That (Lyrics)

In a situation I can't seem to do a thing about

Trouble is knocking at my door

Disappointment lingers – silence seems to shout

Don't know if I can take no more

What I heard and thought I saw were two different things

Which to believe?

When the enemy has so many faces – who's gonna help me see?

Then I cried (Holy, Holy) oh Lord, can you see me?

I'm trusting for you to do what you said

I can't believe it's the same old thing

That's why I call your name

Oh – He heard my cry… Oh- A thousand times

Oh – Now ain't it good to serve a God like that?

~end~

The last question is rhetorical but you can still respond with an

"Amen"!

CHAPTER NINE
"THE SNOODLE REVELATION"
"Your purpose will pull you from the grave." (Dr. Myles Munroe)

What am I called to do? That is the question asked by most people. I say "called" specifically because it denotes a link to an intended purpose – the reason one was created. They say your purpose is linked to the one thing you enjoy doing the most. But, if you're like me, you enjoy quite a few things. They tell me that is my problem – varied curiosity. Sometimes "They" get on my nerves!

According to God's word we each have at least one talent or gift. That doesn't mean you are limited to just one. It just means all God's children have accountability to the degree and level of each gifting. What exactly are those levels? I have no idea.

My daughter grew up watching Veggie Tales – Christian-based videos with storylines and memorable songs that focus on moral challenges and biblical principles. The hosts are "Larry the Cucumber" and "Bob the Tomato". Some of my favorite songs are "The Bunny", "Barbara Manatee", "The Pirate Song" and "I'm So Blue". Think these shows are just for kids? You'd better think again.

One particular video was called *The Snoodles.* This looked into the life of a newly born Snoodle who came fitted with a backpack filled with various items.

He examines his backpack's contents in an attempt to learn his purpose. He discovers he has wings – which makes him think he was meant to fly. But when he expresses this thought concerning his potential to the older Snoodles, he is ridiculed.

"No Snoodle has ever flown!" they scoffed and his failed attempts to fly were met with laughter and disdain.

He additionally discovered colored pencils and a drawing pad. Therefore, he reasoned at least one of his purposes for being created must have something to do with being artistic. This expressed thought was, again, met with harsh mocking and criticism. Not only that, "They" used their colored pencils and drawing pad to draw pictures depicting his failures. These drawings were mercilessly stuffed in his backpack to remind the little Snoodle that he was, is and would never be anything but a failure. Feeling dejected and unwanted - he runs away.

He walked under the heavy weight of others opinions of him. The journey led him to a tall mountain. There he is invited by a kind man to sit by the fire and have a cup of cocoa. The little Snoodle eventually shares the pictures from his backpack which he believed showed who he was. The kind man exclaimed, "No, no – that is not you" and shows little Snoodle a different drawing.

This drawing was nothing like the others. In it, the little Snoodle wasn't little at all. He was leaner, much stronger, armed with his colored pencils, happy and in flight! The kind man could show the little Snoodle the true picture of who he was meant to be because he was his creator!

Little Snoodle now understood that all those gifts in his backpack had a purpose. He learned the other Snoodles had the same gifts but chose to use them to tear down each other. This negativity hindered their flight potential. Apparently, Snoodles were never meant to walk – they were created to fly.

Tears welled in my eyes as I watched this video. With each one that fell, I unpacked a "They" drawing from my spiritual backpack – asking God to replace it with a "He" drawing.

What does this have to do with anything? In a word – Everything!

You have to know that you are the only "you" that He created. And as such, there are unique purposes attached to your life. No person has the divine knowledge to "always" give you instruction and correction - especially when it comes to your life's direction. Walking under man's expectation is weighty!

I share with my daughter what my mom told me. She said, "Ton, the most difficult thing you will have to do in this life is be yourself – there will be many who want to change you – but only to control you. There will be many who want to press you – but only to diminish you. But, fight to be yourself!"

The knowledge of 'Who I am' was wrapped in 'Whose I am'. My circumstances were about to get tougher (I had no idea how tough) and I would need to know without a doubt that my God purposely created, called and had me.

I share this to encourage you to run from the "They"-Sayers and run to God, your creator, for answers about your purpose and daily path directions. Even when you're at "0", pulling out the true drawings will help reinforce you were never meant to walk – you were created to fly!

I still maintain that "They" get on my nerves!

CHAPTER TEN
"ON THE SHELF (AGAIN)"

This faith-walk was no-joke. I had to become sensitive to God's direction – hearing the next move and the next. What was very clear was that my disobedience in any area of my life would be met with swift chastening. The regular folk call it "getting a whooping". So I had to examine myself and move from and out of relationships that were not parallel with the Word. Disobedience blocks communication with God – and I needed that channel open and enlarged at all times. There's no such thing as a little disobedience. I learned that the hard way.

(Insert music for remembering here – I don't know – you choose it!)

Getting my first place was both exciting and eye-opening. It was exciting because I actually had "my" own place. The eye-opening part quickly came into play when after searching diligently for the broom, it dawned on me that I didn't own one – that was my mother's broom!

I was fresh out of college – not that I graduated but because I was "escorted" out due to poor grades. I'd become the lackluster product of following someone else's design for my life. Just when I had got up the nerve and decided to do what I loved, it was too late. I was told my chance at college was blown – that finding a job was my only alternative. I believed it and started my job search.

So, I rented this two-bedroom garage apartment with hardwood floors and thin drafty windows. The kitchen floor was abysmal and the Southern Girl in me who loved to cook was having none of that! This meant I had to redo it myself. The landlord grudgingly agreed to pay for half of the expense.

Stuffing that long roll of laminate diagonally through the windows of my old Toyota-Tercel-Corolla was no easy fete. Hauling it up the rickety stairs would have been impossible had it not been for the assistance of my downstairs neighbor. He was sober (at the time) and gracious enough to lend a hand.

This was the only exchange of this kind that we had. Usually I gave a quick "hello" or "goodbye" as I sped past him and his leering "guests" who sat drinking outside his ground-level apartment. I would pray that I wouldn't trip on those steps and hurriedly lock the doors behind me.

It was here, in my new space, that I had one of my "Come to Jesus" meetings. For those unfamiliar with this phrase, it simply means I had a spiritual epiphany wrapped in a spanking!

Hung up the phone, after speaking with yet another band that disbanded before I could even attend one single rehearsal – this was the third time! Okay, let me back up a little.

I had been asking the "what's my purpose" question for a while. My "departure" from college and sudden thrust into a cannibalistic workforce heightened the sense of urgency to identify what I was supposed to be doing with my life. While at my mom's house, I felt my "calling" was in the music industry – creating, producing and performing.

This worked for me considering ads for band vocalists and front men/women were plenteous.

The audition process would generally go like this:

1) I'd call and get the audition,

2) Show up and sing about 2-3 songs,

3) Leave with a confirmation that I was "in", then

4) Receive the next-day phone call informing the band had broken up!

The last band break-up was the last straw. I was livid – couldn't believe how the same thing happened to me three times in a row. My anger was directed at God as I stomped across my living room towards the bedroom.

"Why won't you let me sing?" I yelled, "You said that's what I'm supposed to do – but now you are blocking me? Why won't you…"

Then "BOOM"… I heard "You can only do it if you do it for me!"

The weight of this great and frightening "sound" enveloped the entire space. It felt as if everything had been swept from around me. There was no sense of the presence any furniture - not the bed, dresser or nightstand. It was just me - I was the only "object" there. I immediately dropped to my knees – facedown- sobbing – terrified - asking for forgiveness. It was a while before I sat up.

This "event" made clear to me the awesomeness of God's power in comparison to mine. I was even more aware of his patient love towards me. He could've struck me down right then and there! In which case you wouldn't be reading this and I definitely wouldn't be writing! I'd like to tell you that I did exactly as instructed – singing only for Him. I'd like to - but that would be lying.

Now, I didn't set out to disobey (who does?). I was on a first date with this fellow at a local bowling spot. He neglected to reserve lanes (trickster) so we had to retreat to the bar/food area. Lo and behold they were doing karaoke!

The host was doing her best to garner some participation. She was an excellent vocalist. My date who knew I sang – only because I was singing when we danced – pointed to me and yelled, "She can sing!"

I gave him the "are you on drugs?" look. Apparently he was or either he was used to that look because he and his other 20-or-so new-found buddies dismissed it with "awe come on" and "yeah, baby do it" comments.

A fleeting thought to "stop" ran across my brain. I dismissed it thinking surely, there would be no problem with my providing harmony on Bette Middler's "The Rose". Besides, the host sang the entire first verse solo. We finished our duet and I returned to my seat. The natives were satisfied and I was safe to just sit and root others on.

The date was ending on a good note because it was ending! We were having a lively conversation as we walked to our cars. Half way to my car and mid-sentence, my voice left. No, kidding – I couldn't make a sound. My date kept asking what was wrong and what happened. A not so fleeting thought "You can only sing for me" burned like a neon sign in my brain. Oh no!

I took my no-talking self home. The next day found me at my mother's trying to mime the entire experience. She stared at me for a few moments then burst into laughter. That was totally uncalled for and no I didn't tell her so. I couldn't have anyways.

Apparently she didn't get that what I did was so very small in contrast to what the "gang" actually wanted me to do. And yes, in retrospect - that was a gang! They exhibited gang-like tendencies by banding together to force another party (me) to fulfill a leader's (my date) desired actions. That's a gang – I was punked by a Karaoke-Gang! (Insert my mother's laughter here).

My voice didn't return for two weeks. That was enough time to get a better sense of what happened. Bottom line – I disobeyed. My rationalization that such a small thing could in no way be considered an infraction on the directive I received was pure crap. Would that I could – I'd lay blame squarely at the feet of the Karaoke-Gang. However since I received the directive – accountability was squarely at my door.

Anyone who knows me would tell you I'm usually always singing or humming. But they would also verify that in gatherings, when it comes to singing (Karaoke especially) you'll rarely see me on stage. It's natural for people to cheer you on towards openly expressing and sharing what they know you love to do. For those who have wondered why I wouldn't – now you know.

God uses a tighter reign on some more than others. It could be attributable to the level of calling on that individual's life or their potential level of falling and subsequent influence on others who would fall with them. I don't know. But my reign was and is pretty tight and I've stayed away from that kind of stage 'til this day. So you can hear me sing "other" songs in my car, in the shower, on the tennis courts, down the halls, while I cook, etc. Until God tells me otherwise, I'll be cheering you on from the crowd!

All I know is that a small degree of disobedience is disobedience nonetheless.

CHAPTER ELEVEN
"DON'T MIND ME – I WAS HIT BY A TRUCK!"

August 28, 2015 Post from Woman, Warrior, Friend Facebook Group : Good morning WWF! A quick testimony to encourage you… It's Friday – God brought us through! Yesterday, after picking my daughter up from school, I let her read my Aunt Stacy Howard Parchel's post. Knew she would get a kick out of it. I explained the post was in response to WWF study on Psalm 138. We stopped at a red light. I recounted to her that day's scriptures – that God stretches out His hand against out enemy's and foe's anger and He saves us with His right hand. Than "CRASH"!!!. We had been hit!... I made sure my girl was okay, quicky checked myself and looked in the rearview mirror. A big truck... a Chevy Silverado! I got out along with a guy in the car in front of us and went back to see the damage. The driver of the truck, an elderly man, stepped out. I asked if he was okay – "yes," he replied. Then I turned my attention to my car. Looked, looked, ran my hands over and under the bumper, opened up my trunk... No Dent – No Bend – No Crack – No Nothing! I turned to the man (who had a stunned look on his face), extended my hand (handshake) and said "Well it looks like God was looking out for both of us today!"... I thanked the other gentleman who also looked

stunned. As we were returning to our cars the gentleman who got out

to help, shaking his head in disbelief, said "I heard it (the crash) –

and I heard you too (our screams). Which brings us to our scripture

for today... Psalm 138:8 The Lord will perfect that which concerneth

me: thy mercy, O Lord endureth for ever; forsake not the works of

thine own hands. ~end~.

CHAPTER TWELVE
"BACK TO THE BEGINNING!"

Okay, so as promised at the beginning of this read, I'm finally sharing how God answered. I know – it's about time you say. And, you're right! (Don't you just love hearing that?) It was all about time.

The most fascinating aspect is that though God answers, neither you nor I can pinpoint the "how" or "why" of the answers or their macro-effects. Nevertheless, I've learned, regardless of the circumstances – no matter how dire - He answers.

No, I didn't get to participate in the show. No, I wasn't able to come to a happy understanding with the representative. No, I didn't invoke a smear campaign to bring to light the injustice of it all. Then, what did I do? What happened? What higher purpose did my disappointment serve?

Simple – it pleased my Lord to use that event - to compel me to write about His history of deliverance – that you who are reading this right now will be encouraged by this truth…

God is Faithful and Just and His love for you is immeasurable!

In short, it was never all about me. He delivered me through this because of His love for you! God uses the trials in our lives as preparation for us to comfort others.

"Ta-Da"!

My hope is that in your reading you've laughed, been comforted and encouraged. Now it's your turn – "tag, you're it" - to be the encourager. Take someone out for coffee and share a testimony - I say "a testimony" because I know you have more than one! I'll close this in the same manner as I close my *Woman Warrior Friend* posts on Facebook –

"Remember, Your Daddy Loves You Today!"

Epilogue…

Oh, so you want to know how the house deal went down… Well, this *God-Designed-Daily-Faith-Walk-Journey* took my faith to depths unimaginable. God would continue showing Himself strong so much so that "no man could get the glory".

He had a plan! It was unbelievable! I'll share it with you in the next book! Get Ready!

"Remember, Your Daddy Loves You Today!"

LaTonya

www.ingramcontent.com/pod-product-compliance
Lightning Source LLC
LaVergne TN
LVHW051818080426
835513LV00017B/2001